Kuth
From: Tina
12/96

AFRICAN
LOVE POEMS
AND PROVERBS

Compiled by
Charlotte and Wolf Leslau

Photographs by
Solomon M. Skolnick

 PETER PAUPER PRESS, INC.
WHITE PLAINS, NEW YORK

*Additional compilation for this
edition by Nick Beilenson*

Copyright © 1970, 1995
Peter Pauper Press, Inc.
202 Mamaroneck Avenue
White Plains, NY 10601
ISBN 0-88088-791-5
Printed in China
7 6 5 4 3 2 1

LOVE POEMS

LOVER'S HASTE

I have no hat on my head,
I have no shoes on my feet.
In what a hurry I am
When I come to thee!

ETHIOPIA

THE MOON ALWAYS FOLLOWS THE SUN

Calm down, little brother,
Time heals all wounds.
No matter how much one is
    weeping,
The moon always follows the
    sun.

Eat your bananas and fresh
    leaves,
And don't cry any more,
Because forever and ever
The moon will follow the sun.

ZAIRE

SONG OF THE RELUCTANT MAID

I said "no," wouldn't you?
I don't want him as my man.
My parents say I have no
  choice,
Like it or not, I'm going to
  wed.

ZIBA

LOVE SONG

I painted my eyes with black
 antimony
I girded myself with amulets.

I will satisfy my desire,
you my slender boy.
I walk behind the wall.
I have covered my bosom.

I shall knead colored clay
I shall paint the house of my
    friend,
O my slender boy.
I shall take my piece of silver
I will buy silk.
I will gird myself with
    amulets

I will satisfy my desire
the horn of antimony in my
     hand,
Oh my slender boy!

BAGIRMI

MOCKING SONG

Tell me, woman, I ask you,
Can your husband dance?
Tell me, woman, answer me,
How does your husband
    dance?

Oh my God, all he can do
Is to sit and eat.
Ever since I married him
He hasn't moved his feet.

Ah, the glutton!

SUDAN

ZULU LOVE SONG

I saw some maidens, those
    from the Southland
Who were carrying the pain
    of lovers in their water-jars.
They came to the lake, and
    poured out the pain.

But back came the Troubler
   Love, he came and he
   trembled.

Drive me, o Troubler, up to
   the Northland,
To seek a maiden whose heart
   is single,

For the heart of these others
   is double and false!
For the heart of these,
   I know, is false!

SOUTH AFRICA

SWAHILI LOVE SONG

O how big is my beloved,
More than all the ones
    I know.
O how lively does my heart
    beat,
When I only see him glow.

Love can never be forced;
Treat it fondly, it will grow!

TANZANIA

Awesome!!!

LOVE DANCE SONG

You're enchanted with this
    girl;
Yes, she has great beauty.
And she should be yours
    always?
Are you this girl's father or
    mother,
Or the God who gave her
    life?

MOSSI

THEY CALL IT "LOVE"

They call it "love, love,"
Slighting its name.
But it's heavier than a stone
For the one who has to
bear it.

ETHIOPIA

NO REMEDY
FOR LOVE

If I have a headache, I have
myself bled.
If I have the colic, I take
some medicine.
If I am seized by the pox,
I go down to the
Hot-Springs.
But where is there help, for
what *she* does to me?

ETHIOPIA

HEARTSONG

Wherever I am,
My heart is with you, my love.
The river can not keep me
    from you.
In my mind's eye,
I see always you, my love.
Nothing can divide us, one
    from one.
My heart sings for you, my
    only love.

ZULU

THE GREATEST PAIN

The hoar-frost on the plain
  of Segaleh makes my
  members shrink,
A ferocious animal has
  devoured my precious
  mule;

What I eat, is lost; my
supplies are exhausted.
All this has happened to me,
but nothing makes me
worry.
I have only one pain, and that
is the absence of my girl.

ETHIOPIA

OF LIFE AND DEATH, AND LOVE AND FRIENDSHIP

My friend, my friend,
  my friend! . . .
At least, my love, let us not
  part!
For in love, there can be no
  separation.
May God spare us the pain of
  separation,
Let us never, never part
  anymore!

Time comes and time passes.
With each night, the voice
   weakens and old age comes
   nearer.

She is a flower, a picture to
   behold,
Nabiha, the daughter of
   Abdal Karim.

Believe me, she is beautiful
   all over.
Her neck is long, and her skin
   is like silk.

ETHIOPIA

LOVE DANCE SONG

My husband, keep me in
   good health;
Be sure I am dressed and fed;
For a woman ages quick, like
   a bean!

MOSSI

SONG OF LONGING

I will never win you;
You will not be mine;
Your love will not be mine.

WHY DO THEY PREVENT US FROM LOVING?

Thy parents should know
    what love is;
They have lived and grown
    old in love.
Why, when it comes to us,
Do they arrange the chains?

They all say to me "Leave it!"
How can she cease to be
   on my mind,
When she has sown the
   naca-plant
In my whole body?

ETHIOPIA

IT USED TO BE

It used to be,
When you loved me,
That I was sweet as honey.

But now your love
Has passed away
And now you call me ugly.

KENYA

A WOMAN TO
HER LOVER

I have painted my eyes,
I have girded my hips.
I am full of the desire of love.
O my handsome lover!
I shall go behind the wall,
And wearing an apron,

I shall help him paint.
I shall mix his plaster
To repair his house.
O my beautiful, slim lover!
I am going to use a thaler
To buy me a kerchief of silk.

I shall put on my best,
To be with him.
O my handsome,
My slim and graceful lover!

GUINEA

LOVE DITTIES

A flash of lightning
Does not quench my thirst;
What good does it do me
If I just see you from afar?

It is the custom of the Somali
To mock a man
Who has fallen in love.

My heart is single and cannot
  be divided,
And it is fastened on a single
  hope;
Oh you, who might be the
  moon!

Until I die, I shall not give
   up love-songs.
Oh God, forgive me my
   shortcomings!

If a potion tastes bitter,
And yet brings relief,
Would you give it up?

SOMALI

PROVERBS

It is the wife who knows her husband.

ASHANTI

You are beautiful because of
your possessions.

BAGIRMI

Leave all women, save your wife, alone.

LIBERIA

The dying of the heart is a
thing unshared.

SOUTH AFRICA

Love is like a baby: it needs to be treated tenderly.

ZAIRE

A woman is like a mimosa tree that yields gum all day long.

XHOSA,
who are fond of chewing gum

Children are the reward
of life.

ZAIRE

To love someone who does
not love you is like shaking
a tree to make the dew drops
fall.

ZAIRE

When one is in love, a cliff becomes a meadow.

ETHIOPIA

Love paralyzes the joints.

CHUANA, SOUTH AFRICA

A wife is like a blanket; when you cover yourself with it, it irritates you, and yet if you cast it aside you feel cold.

ASHANTI

The ties established between two families by a happy marriage are stronger than those of money.

THONGA

Woman without man is like
a field without seed.

ETHIOPIA

Love is a donkey freed of
all tethers.

FULFULDE

If a friend hurts you, run to your wife.

ETHIOPIA

The man who is not jealous in love, loves not.

TAMASHEK

When the heart overflows, it comes out through the mouth.

ETHIOPIA

The tree-knot spoils the axe;
hunger spoils love.

EFIK, NIGERIA

Dine with a stranger but save your love for your family.

ETHIOPIA

For news of the heart ask the face.

GUINEA

Mutual affection gives each his share.

IVORY COAST

Talking with one another is loving one another.

KENYA

With one wife the heart is warmed; with the other wife the kettle is warmed.

GALLA

Absence makes the heart forget.

KENYA

If you marry a beautiful woman, you marry trouble.

JABO (LIBERIA), NIGER

If you can walk you can dance.
If you can talk you can sing.

ZIMBABWE

Hearts do not meet one
another like roads.

KENYA

A house may hold a hundred men, but the heart of a woman has only room for one of them.

EGYPT

Pride and dignity would belong to women if only men would leave them alone.

EGYPT

Quick loving a woman means quick not loving a woman.

YORUBA

It is better to have a disorderly wife than to remain a bachelor.

EWE

Don't be so much in love that you can't tell when the rain comes.

MADAGASCAR

Love is like young rice:
transplanted, still it grows.

MADAGASCAR

The disease of love has no physician.

SWAHILI